A COLORFUL HOME

A COLORFUL HOME

CREATE LIVELY PALETTES FOR EVERY ROOM

SUSAN HABLE

cofounder of Hable Construction

with LUCY ALLEN GILLIS

PHOTOGRAPHS BY RINNE ALLEN

FOREWORD BY JOHN DERIAN

CHRONICLE BOOKS

SAN FRANCISCO

For my sister, Katharine Hable Sweeney

Text copyright © 2015 by Susan Hable.
Photographs copyright © 2015 by Rinne Allen.

Library of Congress Cataloging-in-Publication Data:

Hable, Susan, 1970- author.
  A colorful home : create lively palettes for every room / Susan
Hable, cofounder of Hable Construction ; Photographs by Rinne Allen.
    pages cm
  ISBN 978-1-4521-3740-7 (hardback)
1. Color in interior decoration. I. Allen, Rinne, 1973- illustrator.
II. Title.

  NK2115.5.C6H33 2015
  747'.94—dc23

                    2014036457

Manufactured in China

Designed by Allison Weiner

10 9 8 7 6 5 4 3 2 1

Chronicle Books LLC
680 Second Street
San Francisco, California 94107
www.chroniclebooks.com

CONTENTS

FOREWORD
6

INTRODUCTION
7

FINDING COLOR
INSPIRATION
9

PINK
ROSE
13

GREEN
TREETOPS
37

NEUTRALS
ARROWHEAD
67

YELLOW
CITRUS
91

RED
THORN
121

BLUE
POOL
147

BLACK & WHITE
SALT
173

RESOURCES
202

CREDITS
206

ACKNOWLEDGMENTS
208

It's easy to fall in love with Susan. Looking through the pages of this book, you will understand why.

She is electric. From her outward appearance to her paintings, design work, and home, she lives and breathes color.

Susan embodies all colors all the time. Not just the rainbow—sure, those colors are all there—but let's not forget the golds and silvers, all hues that sparkle or glow with luster, every shade of gray and black, colors that are invisible. She is made up of all of them.

In being so passionate and comfortable with her personal palette, Susan shows us just how easy it is to live with color. Her generosity of spirit shines off these pages. Susan invites us to see how easy and natural and beautiful and exciting it all is; she encourages us to trust ourselves and have fun.

Going through this book, I am reminded of so many lovely shared experiences with Susan that involve just looking at and talking color. I remember last year she came to my house on the Cape and we spent the afternoon combing the beach. She returned home with a pile of small shells, which at first glance all just looked brown and gray to me. But not to Susan. When I looked closer I saw a spectrum of color. Purples, magentas, blues. How did I not see this? Am I color blind? Of course Susan had seen it immediately. This is just one example of allowing oneself to see. In this book Susan shows us where to look and how to open our eyes a little more.

Congratulations, Susan, on sharing your passion for color in all its shades.

John Dr.

INTRODUCTION

As a textile designer and artist, I am surrounded by color every day.

In 1999, my sister Katharine and I began our textile business, Hable Construction, developing a line of fabric designs and products based on my artwork. We started with hand-printed bags and then began selling fabric by the yard. Soon we were known for bright and bold colors and lively hand-drawn designs. We opened our own storefront in New York as the business grew, creating and selling all sorts of products for interiors. Through my design work for Hable Construction, I was able to hone my eye for color. I came to realize that my understanding of color came directly from what I saw in the world around me.

When my family and I decided to leave New York City and move to the small, artsy town of Athens, Georgia, I was faced with a new creative challenge: designing my own home for the first time. Even with my design and art background, I felt overwhelmed by the task.

So what did I do? I went on walks and took note of colors from my new city—blooms, feathers, stones, bark, leaves. I looked to my collection of treasures from my travels to guide and inspire me while I was planning. I extracted textures or overall palettes from these items—the pattern of an antique textile, the general feeling of a collection of artwork, the color in a rug or blossom. As I gathered inspiration, I asked myself these questions: What did I want to live with day in and day out? What mood did I want each space to have? How would I use each room, and more important, how would my family live in these rooms? These are the key things I considered as I collected the colors that would surround us in our home.

Our home is now a place where I live out some of my wildest color dreams. Some rooms are wrapped in one hue from floor to ceiling; some are eclectically layered; some pale and soothing. While each room is grounded in a specific color story, they are also constantly evolving. I frequently shuffle furniture, art, and accessories around, creating new assemblages and vignettes. A lot can change with the addition of a slipcover or a new piece of artwork, or by simply moving decorative pillows between rooms. This fulfills me creatively, helps me appreciate each component, and most of all, makes my home feel, and remain, fresh. I love the challenge of using what I have rather than acquiring a lot of new things, and color sets the tone for what I want each space to achieve.

Much to my amazement, I now work with color full-time. I utilize my expertise when selecting inks for my paintings, composing the palettes of my patterns for Hable Construction, and pulling schemes together for my home. I even analyze color for other creative industries as a board member of the Color Association of the United States. In this role, I discuss color with professionals from many outlets: design consultants, international color trend forecasters, color theorists, reps from the beauty industry, carpet manufacturers, and others. We all share our current color inspirations—from film stills to the natural world to teen pop culture—and predict color trends for interior environments. I love assigning names to our color selections and am especially excited when I see them appear in the marketplace.

As an artist, it is impossible to separate what I do from my daily life. I build color palettes while walking down the street or working in my garden, while playing with my children or dining with friends. When I see a cherry blossom in full bloom, I investigate the details of the bud and the colors in the leaves and stem, cataloguing the palette in my mind. A sidewalk shimmering with mica can provide as much inspiration as a sunset. With this book, I'm most interested in inspiring and encouraging you to trust your instincts with color, as I have learned to trust mine. That's really what it's about. I want to empower you to go for it! Become the artist, and feel confident in placing color in your environment. I hope to give you a foundation in the basics of color, help you discover the hues you are attracted to, and offer ideas for how to utilize them in your home.

In the following pages, the color chapters are named after natural objects, as I believe that one formal color name, like *red*, cannot possibly explain all the richness I see in that hue. The textures and tones of a color are what make it interesting. By walking through the seven palettes—Rose, Treetops, Arrowhead, Citrus, Thorn, Pool, and Salt—you will develop your own understanding of color. The palettes are only a beginning. I'll take you into sitting rooms, studies, bedrooms, bathrooms, hallways, kitchens, guest rooms, libraries, porches, keeping rooms, living rooms, entryways, and even my art studio to show you how you can translate palettes into different spaces. Along the way I suggest things you might do to help your design investigation and invigorate your color experience—visit historic sites, gather fruits and vegetables, group objects you love together. You soon will be able to create pleasing palettes from the scenes in your world and incorporate them into your daily spaces.

Color is instinctive. When you develop a keen sense of color, forming color combinations comes easily. Color can also be intimidating. For those of you who get overwhelmed thinking of all the steps it takes to design a room, my biggest piece of advice is this: Don't be afraid of color. Let it come naturally to you. I'll share some ways I like to approach color and carry it through the design process.

COLOR THEORY

What we call color is actually the product of our eyes and brains working together to process light waves. Color requires light to even exist! Scientists began studying color by quantifying what they knew: A prism refracts light, breaking it into the colors of the rainbow—red, orange, yellow, green, blue, indigo, and violet. Many different people throughout history experimented with these colors and how they work together to create versions of what we today call a color wheel. Color wheels, at their essence, show us how colors can be categorized in relation to one another. A color wheel is a great guide to pairing colors and understanding color combinations.

What the color wheel gives us is an organized diagram of all the colors in the rainbow. Three colors adjacent to each other on the wheel (analogous) almost always work beautifully together, as does one color in varying tints and shades (monochromatic). Colors opposite one another on the color wheel (complementary) create contrast and interest—when of the

same intensity they even seem to vibrate. As you grow accustomed to using color, revisit the wheel often. Come back to it when you're stumped, use it to gain confidence in unlikely combinations, and study it to discover which color harmonies reach out to you.

COLOR GLOSSARY

Primary: red, yellow, blue
Secondary: orange, green, violet
Tertiary: red-violet, red-orange, yellow-orange, yellow-green, blue-green, and blue-violet
Hue: color
Shade: adding black to any hue
Tint: adding white to any hue
Saturation: intensity of a hue from dull to vibrant

Simple Color Schemes

Complementary: opposite each other on the color wheel
Analogous: side by side on the color wheel
Monochromatic: tints and shades of a single hue

ENGAGE WITH YOUR SURROUNDINGS

My garden is the ultimate palette and informs many of my design decisions. It's my ongoing, living art installation. I dig, plant, and move things around all the time to mix things up. The textures, layers, forms, and hues of the natural world never fail to inspire me. It's no wonder there's a history dating back centuries of creating dyes and pigments by hand using natural elements: dirt, berries, roots, leaves, and flower petals. When I truly open my eyes, the color dimensions of my garden are incredible. Roses with striations and layers of pink-to-cream ombré. A porcelain vine with shocking cobalt and turquoise berries that look painted. Long cones of yellow from a butterfly bush, orange trumpets of honeysuckle, fluorescent lime-green shrubs—a bounty of color!

To get comfortable with color, spend time outdoors and log what you see. Think about the combinations that organically occur and how you might bring them into other areas of your life. Observe nature through the seasons. In the winter, the majority of my garden is dormant, so I see stark lines and contrasts, a pattern of neutrals, grays, and browns against whites and blacks. I become more focused on form and silhouette. In the spring, there's renewed energy, hope, and bursts of bright color. Summer's rising temperatures intensify color; the brightness of the sun brings concentration to the blues of the sky and water. Autumn is dusty, warm, and transitional.

You can find color inspiration no matter what your surroundings may be. In New York City I was always looking around, especially on long walks at dusk. There was something about the combination of crowds and reflective glass that always felt vibrant, like a party with a disco ball. In the country, the discovery of a red or gray dirt road or the view of a wide, open meadow can enlighten.

Hone your observation skills: Notice colors, forms, and textures and write down or sketch what you see. Taking photos is an excellent way to collect inspiration; you can even take specimens—petals, twigs, pods, leaves, feathers, shells—home with you. It takes practice to be aware of your surroundings in this way, but it pays off. Big tangles of tumbleweed rounded up in the Texas desert have inspired a Hable textile pattern, as has a collection of seashells. I built the palette for a guest house around stones I plucked from a beach on a family trip.

Being curious keeps you young and alive. You'll never be bored. Being in nature, traveling, researching, reading books—all of these things keep me informed so that I don't have to rely on trends when it comes time to create. Pay no mind to any fear you may have regarding color. There is even a beauty in failure—you will learn that it's completely okay to discard a color that feels off the mark to you. Trust yourself as you research and experiment, and be sure to give yourself plenty of time to develop. The more you experiment, the more you will hone your own style. Once you're comfortable with building your own color combinations, the transition from palette to home won't be as daunting.

There are simple things you can do to train your eye for color. Here are some of my favorite practices:

GATHER	COLLECT	SKETCH
WALK	LOOK	COMMUNE
ENTERTAIN	COOK	TRAVEL
RESEARCH	PLAY	DRIVE
EXPLORE	READ	GROW

BRING COLOR HOME

In my own home, I want color to embrace me, so I use it liberally. I generally begin each room with one color. For instance, I knew I wanted my dining and sitting rooms to be built around a certain shade of pink. Truthfully, it took months of trial and error for me to find the right one. Once I found the shade, I focused on building out the colors of the rest of the room.

I like a lot of different pinks, so I looked to my rose garden in order to get more specific shades. I took specimens from one plant—buds, blooms, and petals—and built a palette from their component colors. This palette was translated into these rooms in layers: paint, floor coverings, textiles, and wallpaper. Then, taking a cue from the stems and foliage, I added green with accents, lighting, textiles, and art. As common a pairing pink and green might be, I wanted the end result to feel fresh and sophisticated. You can see how this palette played out differently in two different rooms in the next chapter.

To develop a palette, first identify the core color. Paint sample colors on heavy paper to use as your backdrop. Throw in inspiration you have gathered—natural elements, swatches from the paint shop, spices, art supplies, antiques—to figure out the combinations you want to create. Live with the collection for a few weeks, observing how the light on the colors changes throughout the day, and swap colors in and out as you see fit. Pay attention to what feels successful. Once you're happy, it will be easy to start translating the palette into a room.

When pulling together colors for a space, I consider the room's location, what the space connects to, and my point of view from other rooms. Color choices can be informed by the colors and textures that peek through from adjacent rooms and windows. I have two approaches to color in a space: minimalist and maximalist. Minimal spaces are white rooms that drop in a burst of color. Maximalist rooms are wrapped in the color, a full commitment.

A monochromatic color scheme can seem intimidating, but it actually achieves a result that is deceptively simple. Because no other colors are present to provide a divergence, this type of palette is naturally serene, calm, and elegant. This effect can be dramatic in its subtlety. Remember to let go of any compulsions you might have to match everything perfectly—trust these tints and shades to work together even if they aren't exactly the same. When you identify the core color for a space, think about how prominent you'd like the color to be before bringing in complements and contrasts.

At the end of the day, choosing a color palette needs to be about the colors that give you a positive emotional response. These are different for everyone. Think about how you want to feel in your space—happy, calm, relaxed, or energized? How will you use each room? To entertain, eat, play, or sleep? Find and use colors that support and enrich your life every day.

PINK

ROSE

I have filled my rose garden with every shade of pink.

It takes a lot of guts to decorate with pink, but don't underestimate this dynamic hue. A color that may seem predictable and one-note, pink can actually be the perfect catalyst to creating a very warm and strong environment. Pink can be wild, bright, and happy (think hot pink, magenta, or fuchsia) or elegant and inviting (think blush or rose). It's versatile and pairs well with other colors, especially gray, taupe, emerald, and chartreuse. I especially love the depth and range of pink and like to layer its many shades from dark to light. Pink is also a flattering color—it's lovely to wear and reflects on the skin beautifully. Have you ever sat in a pink room? It makes everyone glow!

ROSE PALETTE

The pairing of pinks and greens so often found in nature makes for a great pairing indoors, too. The green tempers the pink from being too sweet. Add in some paler tones of the two, and you have a lovely, livable palette.

This palette was inspired by the roses in my garden. I noticed that the dried stems faded to a beautiful shade of green. I had some pigment that mimicked this color, so I added it to the palette in a vintage measuring scoop. A few pastels from the local art store and some watercolors dried in antique porcelain paint pots resemble the range of shades found in the rosebuds. A dash of Himalayan pink salt in the most luminous blush is the perfect complement. I often pay attention to the colors of things in my pantry or at the grocery store—spices and herbs, dried beans or legumes, even flour and grains. Their richness and saturation are unmatched.

In this parlor, the interior walls are very pale and bolder shocks of intense color are brought in with the accents: art, upholstery, and lighting. Even though the room is predominantly pink, the wall color acts as a neutral in this space.

AN IDEA

Do Something Unexpected

If you don't want to go all-out with a bold color, find a way to sneak it in. Don't worry about matching! Go with a burst of color in a surprising place.

On the underside of these daybeds, a large-scale Hable design in a rich magenta contrasts with the neutral, textural seat. This pattern has the largest scale in the room and brings interest to a spot that would commonly be overlooked. This is also a clever way to use a fabric remnant.

I found this faded pink paint color after searching for years for that magical shade that warms a space. It works beautifully for the ceiling of this room and showcases the antique chandelier encrusted with hand-painted leaves.

SHADES OF PINK

I love the kaleidoscopic design of this wallpaper. Kaleidoscopes are rarely monochromatic—remember all the colors when you looked into them as a kid?—so the all-pink pattern is a contemporary take on a classic idea. You'll notice that it does not match the pink rug exactly, but I prefer it that way. This is a great example of how to layer shades of a color together using texture and pattern. Embroidered linen, cotton velvet, and silk jacquard complement a solid rug and patterned walls. Small remnants of rose-colored velvet and a sparkly Moroccan fabric perfectly dress the boudoir chairs. This room also illustrates how fun it is to play with scale. Petite furniture and high ceilings create an Alice in Wonderland effect.

I love this photograph of a Japanese magnolia taken by my friend—and the photographer for this book—Rinne Allen. The print hangs on patterned walls in my dining room. The silky pink color, the haziness, and the magnified viewpoint make it abstract; it reads like a wash of watercolor.

Buy Art

Buy art for your home. It doesn't have
to be expensive; just buy what you
love and are naturally drawn to. Art
can inspire a palette for a whole room
or spark new ideas for color combinations. Go to local shops or galleries to
see what's out there. I always try to
buy from young or new artists to support them. Seeing what other artists
create gives me a different perspective
and energizes my creative process.

PINK AND BLACK WITH SHIMMER

Moody and evocative, graphic black is a seductive partner to pale pink. In this dressing room, black architectural details starkly contrast with feminine wallpaper. The high-gloss black paint on the ceiling reflects natural light—a dramatic use of color. The vintage pink velvet Mardi Gras dress with silver sequins and embroidery works as a showpiece in the room. Fanciful and dreamlike, pink and silver feel magical together.

Don't be afraid to incorporate a little sparkle into your space. You can see a rainbow of colors in luminous strands of sequins—pink, lime, purple, chartreuse, and orange. Reflections supply endless color inspiration, always changing with the light.

This old paint palette echoes the lusterware vase that sits on a window-sill. If you recognize the colors that you love, you will find them repeated throughout your everyday life.

A FABULOUS TANGLE
OF FRINGE AND SPARKLE!

The wild, untamed colors of this costume piece
inspired the palette of the ever-evolving kid's
room, at right.

A LITTLE LADY'S ROOM

I enjoy decorating for kids because their spaces are always changing and you can use so much imagination—there are no rules! Here, in a girl's bedroom, subdued walls soften the environment and a gilded and tufted headboard provides a hint of tradition. These elements are juxtaposed with splashes of neon, bold fabrics, and high-impact art. The room is a success because the pale background makes the details pop. If everything stands out, nothing does!

Roses really are a feast for the eyes and nose—a sensory overload in the best of ways. The tiny boutonniere roses are also delightfully fragrant. The color range seen here is exquisite—even in just one bloom, the most intense magenta fades into the palest pink. The brilliant green leaves, pink petals in varying shades, and yellow centers are a natural presentation of a favorite color combination.

A NATURAL LINE

This recent painting of mine, at left, using liquid watercolor pigments was based on the forms of a dried allium flower. Sometimes I specifically sit down to paint for a fabric design, and sometimes I'm just making art to satisfy my innate need to create. Imperfect and honest, this hand-painted look and feel cannot be duplicated by machines or computers. The irregular line quality of hand painting has become a signature in Hable designs.

One of our first patterns, the Stripe, clearly demonstrates this style. A fabric globe in this design illuminates a dining room. Light fixtures are an opportunity to use color and pattern in an unexpected place.

Collect Things in a Color Story

I think of the treasures I have gathered as the finishing touches that give rooms their unique character. Group finds together based on color, or let an object stand alone. I'm often drawn to certain colors in antique stores, fairs, and flea markets. You simply cannot match the quirkiness and faded glory of old things. Collect things you love and slowly build color stories around them.

TREETOPS

The richest greens are in the canopies of trees.

Since becoming a gardener, I have seen green in a new way. Instead of traditional hues, I now see it in tones and textures of leaves: fuzzy blue-green, shiny black-green, and waxy red-green. Green breathes life into the home—it is fresh air, growth, and promise. It's renewing but also strong and enduring. Think of evergreens clinging to their color in the dead of winter and shoots unfurling through layers of dirt. Green is steadfast. I love the changing palette of greens throughout the year—deep and rich emerald in the winter, clean and sharp kelly in the spring, bold and bright jade in the summer, and fading and dusty eucalyptus in the autumn.

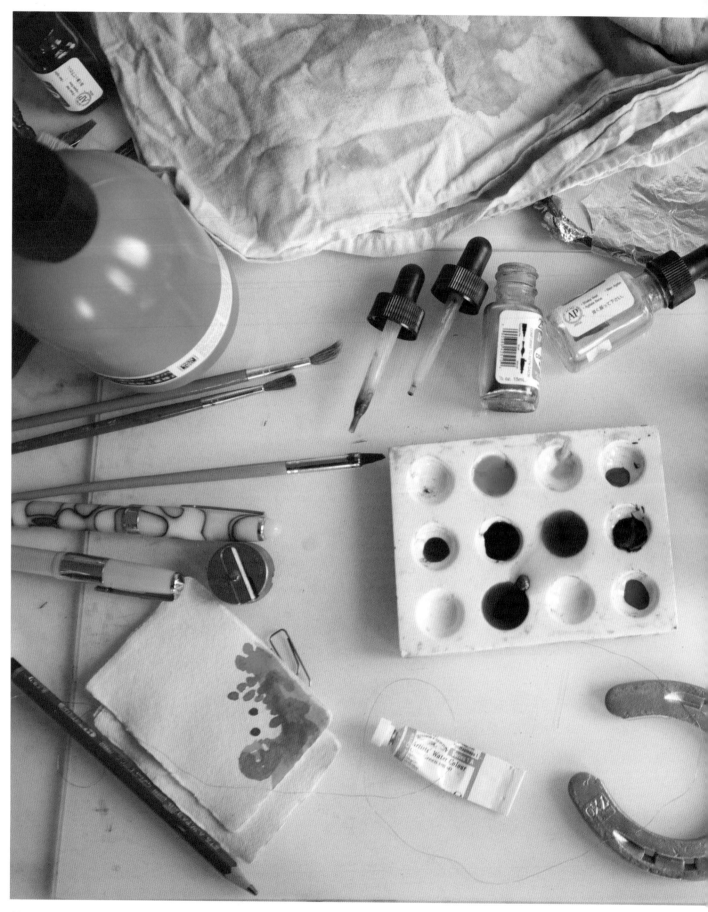

TREETOPS PALETTE

Green provides a crisp backdrop from which to expand your palette. I love to use layers of different shades of green, or pair it with gold, plum, gray, black, or navy. This menagerie of studio tools represents the color's versatility: a painting rag used to mop up a beautiful range of greens, a small watercolor palette of deep and dark colors, gold leaf paper, and gold-brushed horse-shoe and nails. A tester canvas of strokes and dashes in gentler shades reflects the palette's range.

In this small sitting area, at left, tiered shades of green graduate upward from dark to light, giving loft to the ceiling and rooting the floor with earthy browns. Quirky antiques collected over time add character and heart to the space. Creatively painted furniture is a wonderful way to make a color statement, especially on antique pieces, and is something you can easily do yourself.

The deep emerald walls in this guest bedroom show the power of a strong color choice. Complementary flashes of red contrast perfectly with the green—color wheel theory at work!

A GENTLEMAN'S STUDY

This room is full of brilliantly saturated color, similar to the rich colors found in a garden. Using a variety of finishes in the same color family—jade mohair upholstery, glossy leaf trim, matte ivy walls—makes this room a success. Notice that the selection of art is varied: abstract painting, oil portrait, photograph, and drawing. The repeated use of natural materials such as wood, marble, and stone grounds the vivid palette.

AN IDEA

Take a Walk

Walk around your garden or neighborhood or even your local plant nursery. As you go along, snip, sketch, or photograph a unique leaf or flower. Note the colors. Color always changes with the light, too, so make observations at different times throughout the day. I often study specimens to witness their changing forms and colors— budding leaves, full blooms, decaying plants, discarded petals.

Start from the Bottom

When designing a room, I love to work from the ground up. Floor coverings are a great way to incorporate color, texture, and pattern. This rug was one of the first things I bought when renovating my house. I had never seen an Oriental rug with green as a base. I didn't know exactly where it would live, but I knew it would work somehow. This purchase reinforces a good lesson in decorating—if you fall in love with something, you will find a place for it. This particular piece ignited the entire palette for the room: mossy green, wine, and pink with pops of teal and yellow.

The high-gloss door frames the view from the study. It was a considered choice given what you can see through the doors—shades of taupe and metallic gold in the hallway and pink walls in the living room. When choosing colors, consider the spaces you can see from each vantage point in the home.

Layering tones on top of a strong neutral base is a great way to use color. An antique backgammon set from Brimfield market in Massachusetts demonstrates the power of this technique: brown base, ivory dice, green points, yellow chips, green case. It's a multipurpose accent: fun to play but also inspiring and lovely to look at.

A PRESSED PALETTE

My mother frequently sends me flowers that she presses and dries. Their colors fade and shift from what they looked like when they were growing, revealing a natural, washed-out beauty. These pressings have inspired some of my huge ink paintings and the palettes I used in my home. This particular selection presents different dimensions of green—sage, olive, and avocado—with powerful accents of sunflower yellow and cornflower blue, which you can see translated in the room on the following page.

This pale green, blush, and black wallpaper, at far left, has an old-fashioned and proper feel, perfect for a powder room. It references the soft colors of dried flowers and stems. I paired the paper with my collection of tiny paintings of eyes. Bathrooms are fun spots to go out on a limb with decorating because they are a bit more hidden.

AN IDEA

Visit with History

One of my favorite ways to get inspired is visiting historic sites. They open my eyes and introduce me to new stories. I was awestruck after my first trip to Drayton Hall (left), an eighteenth-century plantation near Charleston, South Carolina. This National Trust Historic Site is truly breathtaking. The milk paint, ornamental woodwork, and attention to detail are astounding. It, like many other historic places, proves that things don't have to be predictable or traditional to stand the test of time.

Discover new places by doing some research. Call a local chamber of commerce, search online, or stop by visitor's centers for information on historic homes and sites. You'll be surprised how much there is to discover in your area. I love doing this when I'm traveling, too.

GO BOLD

This home to two artists is drenched in extreme, nonconformist hues. It's almost electric. The owners' motto is "There is no bad color." Remember that! In their son's bedroom, the glossy green door punches through the orange walls and a hot pink coverlet intensifies the overall impact. Gray painted floors and a white ceiling bestow moments of calm, as do the straightforward midcentury furnishings.

Uninhibited colors and strokes emit energy and vibrancy in this watercolor I painted, much like the palette used in the room on the facing page.

LIGHT PLAY

This camellia is actually sitting against the same blue-green wall found in the living room, at right, but as the light in the room changes, so do the colors. Therefore, when choosing a paint color, test large swaths of paint in different areas of your room and observe the effects of the day's changing light. Here, the blue-green walls pair perfectly with wood paneling and warm tones of bark, ivory, blush, and cinnamon from our treetops palette.

TRADITIONAL

These pages illustrate two perspectives on a unique palette. A faux marble–painted mantel executed in malachite green is the focal point of this traditional sitting room, at left. The architectural detail has the illusion of stone, giving depth and weight to the room. The portrait over the mantel is the tipping point; zesty orange is a terrific surprise with the green. Even if the accessories were removed or changed, something I do often in my home, the foundation of the room would still be stunning. Potted plants reinforce the green theme, add texture, and soften edges.

MODERN

Here, smoke painted floors, an aquamarine door, and a dash of tangerine interpret the same palette in a more modern way.

GO BRIGHT

Lime curtains add an electric kick to a multitasking dining, office, and gathering area, casting a green radiance on the room. Flowers, seat cushions, and statement art add pops to the space. If you are going to use one color as a focal point in a room, let it be one that you really love.

AN IDEA

Add Some Life

Plants and flowers bring a living element to a room, brightening the palette and allowing you to experiment with new color combinations. Tending is fun, too: deadheading, watering, rearranging. It's good to get your hands dirty.

Here, varying shades of green sit pleasantly together. A rich burnt-brown trim flanks sage walls. Patina, diffused light, and shadows cast on the wall give this quiet corner in a study intrigue. Breathtaking!

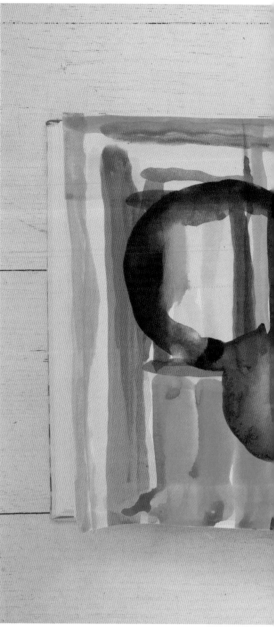

AN IDEA

Keep a Sketchbook of Inspiration

Find a little book with heavy paper that you can paint in. Collect and affix pictures from magazines that inspire you. Doodle or sketch with different materials. Paint or draw color studies based on objects found in your home or nature. Paste in gathered flowers and leaves. Make notes and carry the book with you for a while. A good old-fashioned sketchbook can document your life and the colors of your world like nothing else!

ARROWHEAD

You can find the grand range of neutrals in
arrowheads made from natural materials.

Neutrals are soothing and spare. It's layers upon layers. Colors in this palette are earthy, dependable, and honest: gray, taupe, stone, flax, tobacco, oatmeal, heather, caramel, chocolate. These colors provide relief from the Technicolor modern world. This is an intimate palette that lends itself to tactile elements: shorn sheepskin, rocks, bark, driftwood, sand, a well-worn cashmere sweater. Neutrals also make a great backdrop for hanging art. They draw the walls back and let the objects move forward.

ARROWHEAD PALETTE

Neutrals are simple, and you can build depth with them by layering textures— tone on tone, shine on matte. Adding in hints of pale blue or gray, as I have done here, is a way to bring in color surreptitiously. A worn rope, a hand-forged hook, an old concrete weight, a tiny metal bowl, a flat stone, handmade rough watercolor paper, black India ink, and a metallic sponge each bring textural interest. Deep pewter anchors the soft neutrals. This is a calming palette with a lot of possibility.

Gray neutrals lay the groundwork for a serene space to harbor weary travelers in this cottage. The Hable Ribbons fabric on the bedspread is an example of how details in a charcoal shade can enhance neutral surroundings, such as the Swedish gray of the stained walls.

I collected these rocks from a beach encrusted with smooth stones as far as the eye can see in Provincetown, Massachusetts. I scooped one up in every shade of gray, from light to dark. They inspired the palette in the guest house and sit out as a reminder of summertime spent with friends and family.

AN IDEA

Travel

Visit a lake, desert, forest, beach—any new environment distinct from your own. When I think of the places I have traveled, so many color memories come to mind, from the creamy limestone of my childhood summer camp to the amber sands of the Sahara desert I saw as a young adult, to the white sand beaches of Florida, where I like to go with my family. When you travel, your eyes are open to the less familiar surroundings.

This still life brings together key elements for a neutral palette: gray walls, wood, a deep amber glass bottle, and a hint of color in the form of the sculptural green allium stem.

The bedroom at right is tawny and eclectic. Chocolate, taupe, buttermilk, and caramel mix together to create an inviting place to rest. A wall of neutral but dynamic art is simultaneously peaceful and stimulating. Neon touches—necklaces, feathers, brooches, and hair ornaments—are pinned up on display, adding a cheerful note.

Neutrals pale and deep sit together in this room. Creamy walls and shelves envelop books, family photos, antique baskets, and regional pottery. I love how the baskets sit on their sides to show off more detail. Try cleverly arranging heirlooms and keepsakes to show off their best angles.

Eggs, acorns, pecans, cotton, you name it: An outdoor harvest is sure to yield a bounty of neutral colors that could be your next source of inspiration. Look up what's in season and go out to gather. It's a perfect way to discover new combinations. This day's pick of Araucana chicken eggs presents an ideal color scheme. I would take these beauties into my local paint store and ask them to custom-match paint for each one!

You can see some of the creamy eggshell colors in these fabrics. Pillows made from a worn rag rug and a Bolivian blanket exhibit a faded pastel palette that brings tints to the neutral space.

AN IDEA

Transition with the Seasons

Work with the palette that nature delivers throughout the year. In the winter, I change my interior spaces to echo the less vibrant colors outdoors. I have thick, nubby linen slipcovers for my blue sofa and cushions that blanket the room in soft neutrals. Creating a very different look and feel, this austerity is nice after long seasons of lush color.

NEUTRALS + METALLICS

The repetition of these Moroccan brass globes down the center of an entry hall, opposite, leads the eye onward. When illuminated, the pendants cast golden rays of light in all directions just as the branches of tinsel dance with light and shadow. Attention-grabbing metallics expand neutrals with their shimmering glow. This combination is easy to incorporate into your décor since the outcome is subtle and stylish, not gaudy.

Tree bark glows on a chilly, stark day. Bare trees create incredible forms and colors that can inspire layers of wood and natural tones inside the home for an organic vibe.

Like a winter garden's structure of bare limbs and bark, this raw interior of a guest house, at right, is a spare starting point on which to build a room. The Swedish gray floors, ceilings, and walls completely define the space.

Because the palette is strict, the rest of the design came easily. The textiles were first: The chocolate Hable for Hickory Chair Pom Pom fabric dresses the sofa, and a natural jute floor covering adds great texture. Warm wooden furnishings sit nicely with the cool undertones of the overall gray. The rest of the colors are largely neutral, including the wooden tripod lamp and vintage leather trunks. The sharp jolts of azure blue are the highlights of an otherwise subtle palette.

AN IDEA

Adorn

Ornate accents always work with neutrals. They give sparkle and shine and
create visual interest without over-
powering a space like a color would.
Play around with warm tones like
bronze or copper or cooler ones like
silver or pewter. They're all gorgeous
and easy to incorporate—a lamp
here, a picture frame there. Don't be
afraid to mix them in a single room as
shown in this seating area, opposite.

Rich chocolate velvet chairs hug a cool,
bluish-gray corner in this sitting room.
Alpaca stripes and Turkish rugs ground
the warm furnishings. The golden tones of
the coffee table and lamp balance the cool-
ness of the walls. These shades, partnered
with sophisticated accessories—Peruvian
pom-pom tiebacks, a gold lusterware tea
set, and a silver-framed photograph—yield
a powerful yet welcoming look.

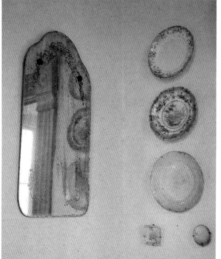

MAKE A SPLASH

The many different shades of gray give this space, at left, a coastal vibe. Serenity comes from the violet and blue family, which brings to mind the air, mist, and fog of the coastline. Adding a touch of color to this palette can have an incredible effect. These splashes of watermelon, azure, nectarine, and lime take the grays into more playful, less serious, territory.

Strips of dyed ash hang on the wall in ombré gray, coral, and rose. You can see how these colors translate beautifully to a finished room.

LAYER

Animal habitats are fascinating; they are created purely out of necessity using foraged materials. Birds' nests are intimate, cozy, and secure. Take a cue from nature's architects and pile on layers of earthy tones and texture—jute rugs, baskets, hemp, and textiles. This sitting area, at right, shows the power of blended neutrals: cool and warm, rough and smooth. It's a cozy nest in its own right.

YELLOW

CITRUS

Citrus is a bold pleaser of the senses.

Uplifting, charismatic, playful . . . this warm palette of gold, lemon, jonquil, peach, coral, amber, lime, champagne, and saffron sings of sun on your skin, ripe fruits, and vibrancy. We see these hues at sunrise and sunset, in seashells, autumn leaves, citrus fruits, and burning embers.

A citrus-based palette feels friendly and inviting. Shades in this family are especially opulent when used texturally, such as in shimmering velvet or smooth lacquer. Cooler hues like turquoise, green, and black bring balance and contrast to a room decorated in a sunny palette. Discriminately placed citrus details—flowers, fruit, artwork—can steal the whole show.

CITRUS PALETTE

This palette feels sunbaked with amber, coral, pale yellow, bronze, and sunflower. The dried bean pod was pocketed from a trip to the Arizona desert and, together with the dried pigment in raw umber, brings in light and dark contrast. Hand-dyed thread and crystals of natural gum arabic from the art store contribute shades of apricot and ginger. Slivers of green in the bottle label and the sunny yellow price sticker stand out as more saturated takes on citrus.

Optimism abounds in this sunroom, all because of a restrained use of a pleasant color scheme. There's strength and cohesion here. A buff-colored dried garlic pod and a bisque flea-market sculpture give texture and accent to the neutral planked walls, linen side chair, and warm wooden tabletop. A delectable pillow in a woven Hable Stripe brings in light citrusy colors and resembles Neapolitan ice cream.

The peach, citron, copper, blush, and white found in this Haitian religious wall hanging transport me to the tropics. I see sherbet-colored row houses, warm sunny days, and tropical fruit. Every culture uses color differently, and it is enlightening to study people, places, and things beyond what we know. This exposure can lead you to vibrant color combinations you may not have thought of before.

Again, we see how citron and peach pair well on this staircase detail, opposite, in an incredible abandoned house near Athens, Georgia. The colors work together because they both have luminous golden undertones and are color wheel neighbors.

LET IT SHINE

Dots of light cast from a disco ball sitting in a low corner of this room, opposite, spontaneously flicker against the ornate ceiling. The movement of light draws your eye up. Peach, nutmeg, and vanilla mix together with the orangey light in this foyer, a pleasing blend of old and new.

Twinkle lights cast a warm glow in any space; they bring atmosphere without requiring a big investment. A bonus: They go up and come down easily. The blurred goldenrod spots remind me of lightning bugs and a summer evening. I like to use them all year-round.

Shades of sky blue and sunshine yellow appear to be grabbed from a clear spring day. The Welcome Center in Athens, Georgia, is styled true to its nineteenth-century era with a color palette that stands the test of time. The focal point, a bright citron sofa, adds zest and balance through its minimal, solid form. Take your favorite kind of day and create your palette around the sky, light, and trees.

LEMON YELLOW

Yellow and orange picked from a clear autumn day are translated into a boy's room, opposite. These colors' cheerful presence parallels a little boy's sunny disposition; the overall feeling is playful and bright. The Hable Ropes curtains tumble with pattern in the sunshine. Don't be afraid to layer tones of citrus—pale lemonade walls and brighter pineapple accents work well together. Stripes of blue, violet, and red in the contrasting rug anchor the room.

AN IDEA

Gather Leaves

Kick up leaves and collect your favorites. You'll see all of the different colors that foliage holds: honey, bittersweet, salmon, saffron, apple green, and persimmon.

A SOFT GLOW

A lemon resin candleholder basks in daylight. Yellow fortifies a moody backdrop. Turn up the volume in a space with citrus hues.

The beauty of hellebores satisfies my longing for blooms when it is still cold outside. This specimen is particularly exquisite, aglow in pastel tones of grapefruit, avocado, and copper with curry-colored stamens.

This gilded corner of a living room is a dreamy approach to the citrus palette, showing off magnificent golden tones, opposite. Creamy walls resemble frosting, and hints of gilt and black take the room to a sophisticated place. Texture and ornament are used abundantly here in a shiny mirror, fluffy tassel, and grainy wooden chest.

A hand-blown Murano glass chandelier cascades light over a kitchen island, casting a copper glow.

When you have a restricted palette, you are able to select your pattern with intention, creating a rhythm to your room. I consider scale and design, but color is the most important thing when finding the right patterns for a space. This nineteenth-century golden entry, opposite, adheres to this rule. It uses pattern in abundance, but the stenciled floor, patterned wallpaper, and painted staircase are all shades of butter yellow, cream, pale cantaloupe, and walnut.

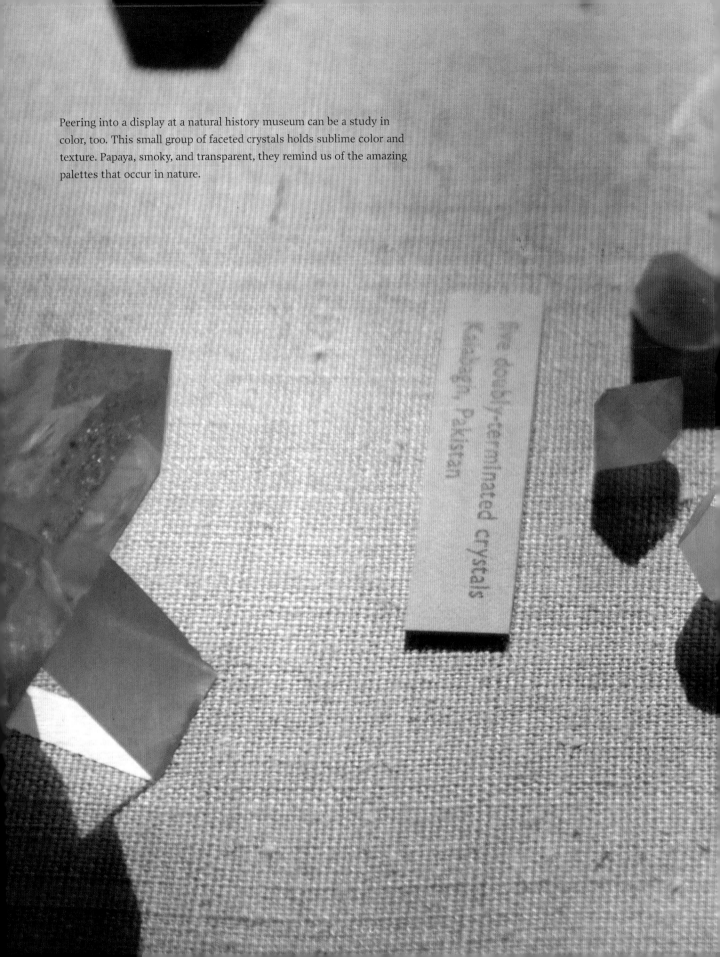

Peering into a display at a natural history museum can be a study in color, too. This small group of faceted crystals holds sublime color and texture. Papaya, smoky, and transparent, they remind us of the amazing palettes that occur in nature.

Fine doubly-terminated crystals
Kashbagh, Pakistan

Watch the Sunrise

Wake with the sun! Experience dawn in all its glory and take note of the different hues that a sunrise holds. The colors change quickly, and sunrise typically treats us to so many shades of yellow, pink, and purple. Taking color from this magnificent daily occurrence and using it as inspiration for your interior can be magical.

This is a beautiful presentation all wrapped up in highly textured, uniquely patterned historic walls. During the building's renovation, existing cracks in the walls were patched with tinted pigment. This process created a strong abstract pattern of gold sunbursts against the remnants of aged blue paint. Against the wall, a collection of vintage suitcases and guitar cases are grouped casually with leaning works of art. This is a great way to test artwork in a space before you commit to hanging.

A citrus palette plays out in limey stems and translucent cameo-colored petals. These Japanese anemones stretch to the sun.

Play with Color

Whether you play around with confetti, glitter, sequins, bubbles, hula hoops, or bouncing balls, having fun can lead to amazing color inspiration. This burst of confetti inspires a playfully colorful palette that works well in a tiled bath.

A SPECTRUM OF COLOR

Swatches of bold color make for a painterly range of weathered tangerine, terra-cotta, gray, celadon, and cyan in this bathroom. The finishing touches of a richly stained trim, modern sink, and blue glass pendant lamps (with blue bulbs!) make the space feel uninhibited. Bathrooms are a great place for playful color, floor to ceiling.

THORN

When I think of red, the thorns on my climbing roses come to mind instantly.

Red is assertive, seductive, and full of body. It signifies ripeness and bounty. In the garden, reds are found in all shades from deep burgundy buds to bright red berries and maroon-tinged leaves. I often gather inspiration for this palette from the kitchen—peeling an apple, biting into a plum, cracking open a pomegranate, cutting beets, drinking wine. Translating this into my home, I prefer to use claret as a lush and powerful embellishment. The color's impact is undeniable.

I love pairing red with white, green, black, and lavender. The lavender might come as a surprise, but this is a natural combination—think of the shades you see in plums, figs, and lilacs. These are analogous colors (side by side on the color wheel) so they work together seamlessly.

THORN PALETTE

Red is powerful. Spread onto the one-hundred-year-old floor of my studio, dried melon-colored rosehips pulled from a vine of climbing roses sit next to pots of vibrant red inks, scraps of paper with evidence of tints and color mixtures, remnants of orchid watercolor in a jelly jar, and a spiral of vintage cherry-red straight pins. Green leaves and traces of dark ruby, black, and white round out the composition.

Take notice! Claret emphasizes different areas of this room. A cushion here, a footstool there—it's impossible for this color to fade into the background. Red reaches out to grab your attention from a sea of striped textiles, layers of stacked books, carefully placed objects such as the childhood dollhouse with its blazing red chimney, and furniture such as the red lacquered coffee table. Using red sparingly and strategically can bring focal points and strength to an eclectic and playful room such as this one.

AN IDEA

Embellish

Having a defined palette makes it easy to embellish a space over time. Add color through pillows or small bits of upholstery like the fireplace stools in this room. Envision a simple paint job on the legs of a table, or place a stack of books in complementary hues on your coffee table.

TONE IT DOWN

A hand-blown glass vase in muted garnet situated in a corner of my studio is a hint that quiet color is attainable and still luscious in this palette. The amethyst-colored sea fan and purple flowers accent the whitewashed walls, chocolate door, and antique seafoam grain bin used as a table. Gorgeous light filters through the window, making this gemstone palette gleam.

Be Brave with Color!

Paint a wall of bookshelves claret and relish in the effect. Using this color so boldly requires courage and confidence in the statement. A similar, slightly subtler trick is painting the inside lining of your shelves; it makes objects stand out. This room gets extra points for the red window trim and red patterned curtains. Bring red into your home and show off your tenacity!

Here we see two takes on a classic theme: black and white with a hint of red. The red is used sparingly, but it is the pulse in both of these settings. A good way to add a touch of energy in a study or quiet space, red can liven up a room without overwhelming.

Talk about going bold—a cardinal-red ceiling cloaks this room in a Victorian home. The paint job stops at the picture molding, not at the wall seam; a smart trick that draws the eye down the walls.

A TAPESTRY

A Navajo weaving from the 1920s hangs in a stairway. Display blankets and remnants of colorful textiles throughout your home for inspiration and texture. Even when your collection is from different places, time periods, and cultures, the color can be the force uniting them—in this case, red!

In this hallway, an arrangement of Chinese lacquer makes a compelling statement in red. The forms create pattern and dimension, and with that lacquer finish, color virtually drips down the walls.

A pine-walled guest bedroom is a comfy and warm retreat. The claret color particularly holds its own here against rich stained wood due to the similar intensities of color. The overall effect is strong yet cozy. Shiny vermillion lamps and antique crewel coverlets complete the look.

A red Chinese chair stands at attention on a peacock-blue painted floor in this foyer, making a color statement in a corner that otherwise may have been overlooked. Take the opportunity to use adventurous color in small areas of your home.

Burgundy and lemon-lime undertones brighten the lavenders and blues in this bounty of freshly picked figs. This seamless blend of colors from nature translates well into the palette of the space on the opposite page. It's another reminder that neighboring colors (in this case, red and plum) on the color wheel work well together.

This image beams red. Hand-stitched and beaded, these hand-shaped objects are created for Mardi Gras in New Orleans by the group called the Mardi Gras Indians, who are famous for their voracious costume-making and lavish parade routines. I am attracted to the extreme graphic pattern and varying shades of claret as well as the tiny beaded texture of the amulets—eye-catching for a flamboyant celebration or room!

My eye stops every time at this jar of homemade jam in my kitchen, which beams raspberry when the sun hits it. The light reflecting through the Mason jar is so beautiful that I haven't wanted to put it away. Now a permanent vignette, this jar of jam is transformed by sunlight into something to behold.

An unexpected selection for a sunroom, a fuchsia-, cranberry-, and sable-striped Peruvian blanket covers an ornately carved antique French daybed. The thorn palette is continued with a painted wine floor and peek of red from the room next door.

AN IDEA

Pick Fruits and Vegetables

Farms where you can pick your own fruits are wonderful places to find colors. Buckets full of blackberries will leave your fingertips claret-stained from the gathering. Apple and peach orchards or pumpkin patches also bring rich palettes to life. Bask in the opportunities that each season brings. Take a friend or two, explore the country, and bring your bounty home to use for color studies.

I am drawn to this still life of incandescent red currants with dark bull's-eyes. Fruits in season are mouthwatering, and the color, flavor, and fragrance are irresistible. Berries, figs, pomegranates, and currants all have striations of every tone of red: claret, plum, scarlet, and ruby. Juicy and rich, they often stain a counter, glass, or hand and leave a lasting impression.

POOL

*The depth of water perfectly represents all
of the varying layers of blue.*

Blue is airy and light. It's not at the root of anything; it surrounds us. It is water and sky, reminiscent of a clear, perfect day, a beach holiday, a rain puddle, dusk. A blue room invigorates me, like diving into a pool of water.

It's a color that is a strong starting point for a palette that emphasizes wanderlust and life. Cobalt, navy, turquoise, sky, aqua, pale, electric, indigo, and lapis—I'm a lover of most blues.

POOL PALETTE

I often reach for blue first when I'm working. Gathered in my studio, these objects are bits of the art supplies that I use on a daily basis: some blue pastels, paint, feathers, melon-colored string, and zesty orange pigment. I threw warmer shades into the palette to show how a small contrasting element can be incredibly impactful. Revisit the color wheel to see how opposites attract. Blue and orange are natural opposites, so a shade of orange makes sense to try first. Remember that you do not have to stick to steadfast rules. Yellow, peach, and black are also great companions to blue.

This room's natural feel takes advantage of the prominent windows and the proximity to the backyard. A blue-green paint shade brings to mind the grass and sky directly outdoors. The color and pattern in the drapes reflects a strong pacific blue, while the tufted lichen slipper chairs favor the soft greens of the landscape. Objects collected over time expand the palette and add tactile color tiers: an indigo *shibori* kimono, a rust antique African mat, multicolored pillows. The finishing touch is a weathered opera prop—a funny wooden wave featuring many different shades of blue.

Here you can see the power of cyan against stark white. The translucence of the watery color in this paint pot and glass pendant lamp, opposite, echo each other. Reflective surfaces enhance color and add luminosity and airiness to the home.

MINIMALIST COLOR

This simple master bathroom, opposite, is an example of careful, restrained use of color. The blue antique pendant lamp radiates against the classic white marble and white fixtures. Don't be afraid to go for an all-white room. Adding a hit of a favorite color can have real impact in the space. In this particular case, the blue reflects the colors used in the rooms close by. Color connectivity in the home is essential to the harmonious flow from room to room.

MAXIMALIST COLOR!

Another way to go is blue everything: walls, ceiling, trim. If you love a color, sometimes you just have to go for it. This laundry room, opposite, glows blue. This is a space where one spends a lot of time; the color is so pleasant that mundane household tasks are made more enjoyable. The subtle aqua accents in the rag rug enhance the all-over color and give the space texture. Minimalist and maximalist color work in spaces big and small.

My bedroom has windows on three sides that look out to the sky. My headboard and bedding are made in periwinkle washed linen, and the walls are painted a muted gray-blue. In designing the color of this Hable Bird fabric, I chose a pale cornflower blue to work with the paint and bedding. A bedroom is a nice place to be surrounded by softer color. Powdery shades make me feel relaxed and safe. I love my sleep, and these types of colors help me fall into it!

The upbeat orange gives this color palette energy! The intense color contrast of the blues and oranges in this sitting room make it eccentric and inviting. The highly textured blue walls, which are an original feature of this historic home, define the space. A benefit of old walls is the inherited distress, which is possible to replicate by stripping paint. On the floor, the Moroccan rug takes a room that could be monochromatic and gives it life. Crackled navy leather side chairs and a worn cream sofa keep with the aged character of the room.

AN IDEA

Curate

On the mantel, the stacks of books and art objects play out the color theme—these books were chosen from a collection for the varying blues of their spines. Both decorative and functional, books can be culled from your own collection to enhance any palette.

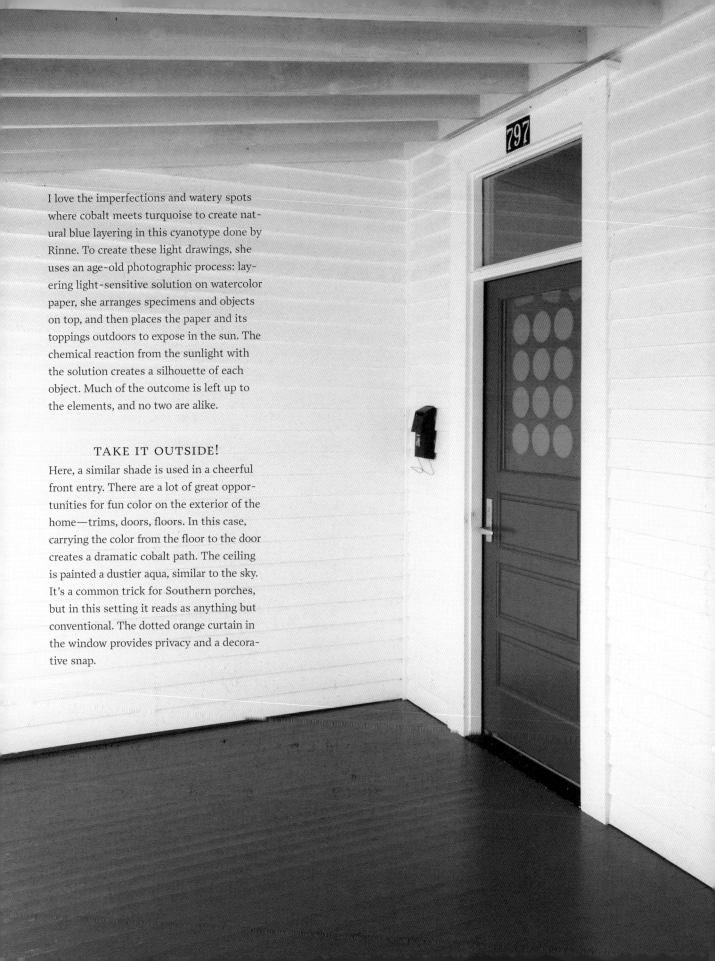

I love the imperfections and watery spots where cobalt meets turquoise to create natural blue layering in this cyanotype done by Rinne. To create these light drawings, she uses an age-old photographic process: layering light-sensitive solution on watercolor paper, she arranges specimens and objects on top, and then places the paper and its toppings outdoors to expose in the sun. The chemical reaction from the sunlight with the solution creates a silhouette of each object. Much of the outcome is left up to the elements, and no two are alike.

TAKE IT OUTSIDE!

Here, a similar shade is used in a cheerful front entry. There are a lot of great opportunities for fun color on the exterior of the home—trims, doors, floors. In this case, carrying the color from the floor to the door creates a dramatic cobalt path. The ceiling is painted a dustier aqua, similar to the sky. It's a common trick for Southern porches, but in this setting it reads as anything but conventional. The dotted orange curtain in the window provides privacy and a decorative snap.

This guest bath is wallpapered with old maps to welcome traveling visitors. The blue of the maps' bodies of water is familiar and comforting, and the collage of maps creates a lovely smattering of blue around the room. Neutral fixtures keep the focus on the color. You can do this with any type of paper, from old book pages to blueprints, by using a decoupage medium and a brush and squeegee. Consult with a local expert at the hardware or art-supply store for ideas and application advice.

This ceiling view, at far left, shows a perfect color balance. The combination of complementary colors in muted tones blended with rich textures creates harmony. The palette smartly utilizes color from the reclaimed wood to inform the color of the window trim. If you have a nook or a room that needs some personality, painting or staining architectural features is a great way to inject color into a space. The light fixture and drapes add layers and pattern without stealing the show.

In this beautiful breakfast area at left, Hable Ropes fabric swims around the banquette, echoing the forms of the trees beyond the windows. The vintage light fixture is fashioned from a wire cage filled with Austrian crystals; the geometric circles give balance to the abstract print.

OPULENCE

These antique tassels and velvet box are luscious. I love to adorn with
texture and shine. The room opposite channels this combination
with honey details and blue walls in different shades. The wallpaper
creates subtle movement. Texture is abundant: a red velvet-lined lid,
an antique textile-lined tilt-top table, carved wooden boxes. Winding
and gestural, the silhouette of the snake is repeated in the embroidery
detail of the tabletop.

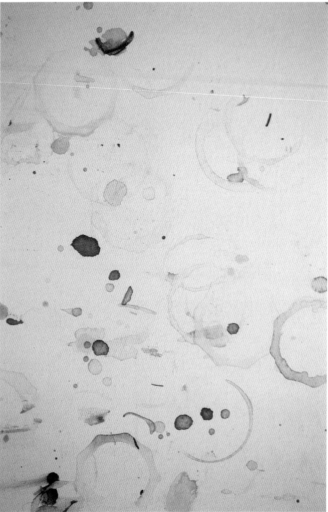

This bedroom, at left, demonstrates an unconventional take on the palette, inspired by the abstract artwork on display. An aquamarine door is sandwiched between cool stone gray walls and floors, a starburst in a sea of neutral. Pink bedding sizzles under a pale blue coverlet and an orange lamp shines on the metal side table.

Flecks of oranges, pinks, and aqua colors picked up in this room—are found in these rings organically created by the jelly jars that hold my watercolor paints. They're a product of my work, another happy accident that sparks inspiration.

I found this little blue case in a Texas antique store, and my son packs his toys and treasures in it when we travel. It kills me; it is so sweet. The rocks are a current passion of his and the subtle differences in their colors, their monochromatic palette, feel transcendent. The painting, opposite, sits in my studio and echoes the colors found in this collection.

AN IDEA

Look to Your Belongings

When you are putting together colors for your home, gather four or five of your favorite objects. You will begin to notice that you have natural affinities for certain colors. Extract four or five colors from this group of objects to ignite a palette.

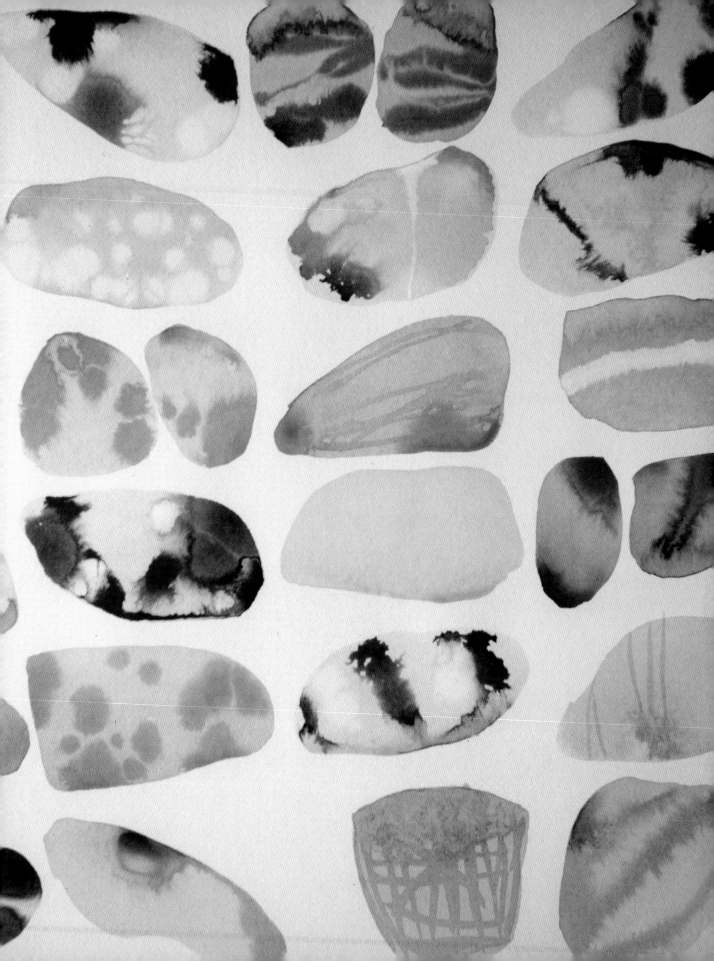

SALT

The irregular crystals of pure salt grains convey the compelling relationship between uncomplicated black and white.

The black and white pairing is crucial for design. Pale and dark, light and heavy, good and evil, absorption and reflection—this is a palette that tells an enduring story of opposites. I often rely on black and white to begin the design process.

Used individually, black and white both project power and sophistication. Black sends a strong sign to be taken seriously; it means business. In the home it feels chic, glamorous, mystical, sexy, moody. On the other side of the coin, white is pure, innocent, and new. A crisp white room creates a clean slate from which to start designing. When used intentionally as a design element, white, like black, is daring. It can feel futuristic, spare, and serious.

Paired with jolts of color, black and white can easily fade from the spotlight; they highlight and frame components of a room beautifully. White gives loft and black gives weight. Look to the minimalist and abstract art movements, checkerboards, and the animal world to witness the dynamic effect of this palette.

SALT PALETTE

Seashells become lovely salt cellars in my studio. Gray-dyed jute on a roll, India ink, and vintage porcelain paint pots live alongside white watercolor ink and the charred edge of bundled sage.

Always powerful, black and white are equally dynamic together or alone. Presented on an old marble tabletop, this palette needs a variety of tones to keep from being too stark. Notice the different whites. Layering whites, blacks, and grays gives important dimension to this simple combination.

My art studio is creamy white, and I couldn't have it any other way. My days are filled with color while I work on different projects—designing, painting, planning, brainstorming. White is light and airy and gives my mind the space I need to create. Black desks and task chairs ground the room.

The matte finish of whitewashed paint is what gives this room a lofted feeling. To attain this warm white, pay attention to the saturation of your paint. The finish you choose will either absorb or reflect light, which can lift a room or close it in. High-gloss walls draw your eye up and add major impact, while a more matte, eggshell paint has a softer appeal for open spaces.

AN IDEA

Read

Learning is the best form of inspiration. Stacks of magazines and piles of books flank my studio walls. I'm always adding them to my shelves. The titles are from many different disciplines, but most are design-related. I also regularly visit our public library to dig through sections that might hold a nice surprise. Surround yourself with publications that will open your mind.

This butterfly collection shows a beautiful range of creamy and pearlescent whites, with similar hints of deep greens and wooded tones found in the porch, opposite.

This porch is painted top to bottom in a deep Charleston-green paint. This backdrop helps lead your eye to the flowers in the yard beyond. When the days are warmer, a porch can be used like an additional room of the home. Switching out the throw pillows depending on the season is an easy way to change the feel of a living space. The weathered table and set of old chairs warm the minimalist palette. The fluted white enamel shade adds interest from above.

A sepia watercolor of a maypop vine of mine hangs in a neutral sitting room, at right. Quiet spots to think are necessary in my color-infused life. A sprinkle of cumin and cinnamon stripes brings a low-impact dose of color to this calming space.

Above, drums are perched in a cubby above a natural wooden door. Warm accents of aged pine are gorgeous and inviting with a clean black and white palette.

TEXTURES IN WHITE

A restored intricate medallion adorns this ceiling at Drayton Hall in Charleston, at left. The highs and lows of the relief form shadows, bringing pleasing dimension to the all-white motif.

Similarly, an heirloom candlewick bedspread made by hand and found at the Brimfield market in Massachusetts features gorgeous texture and pattern in snow-white. I adore the cotton knots and cut pom-poms. When going for all-over white, look for ways to layer with tactile elements.

Artfully hung ebony accents can bring strength to a room. These antique black lacquer bowls are powerful, but interspersing them with a collection of watercolors in muted colors makes for a compelling gallery wall. I love how the two collections form a striking checkerboard pattern. The warm textured sand wall and emerald frames root the collection.

The Hable Trellis pattern seen on this chair is based on the simple black and white drawing of mine, above. The line work of the rendering was so strong and the contrast so stark, I knew it would make a distinctive fabric. A refurbished antique chair in black lacquer frames the design and brings masculinity to the pastel, wildflower-covered walls. The layering of patterns works here because of the contrast of stark black and white against soft colors.

SHADES OF WHITE

Many shades of white are represented in this abandoned church. Its current glory of peeling white paint, almond ceiling, alabaster pews, and milky pendant lights inspires. The layers of whites in this context hint at ghostly memories of christenings and marriages, white gloves and white dresses. Blending whites can be achieved in the home by layering linens, varying paint finishes, and decorating with porcelain and ceramic vessels featuring different white glazes.

This Austrian pirate ship light fixture is one of my favorite finds, spotted at a Texas antique fair. It is perfectly silhouetted against the stark white entry. Hand-forged black iron hanging from whitewashed wood evokes strength, while the ship brings an element of playfulness and adventure. Sometimes one incredible detail is all you need to liven up a space.

In this dining area, at right, a disciplined palette is grounded in black and white. The vintage African blanket enlivens a tabletop with its strong pattern. An antique Chinese screen panel hung on the wall resembles an open shutter and makes the windows appear larger. Driftwood-gray chairs, a handmade cotton wreath, a pine cupboard, and straw baskets add doses of nature and neutrals. The brass light fixture and unconventional black cups and saucers marbled with metallic gold add shine.

White on white in geometric shapes is a study of form pieced together with artist tape in the studio. It was originally intended for a multicolor pattern, but the result was so crisp in all white that it stayed this way!

TAKE THE EDGE OFF

Soften crisp white with natural wooden details. Lightly stained reclaimed ceiling wood, penny tiles, milk glass pendants, and hand-plastered walls bring in nice lines for your eyes to follow in this inviting bathroom. The finished product is angular and sharp but still feels warm because of the textures, natural trim, and pale aquamarine accent wall.

Sunlight reveals the intricate detail of these spectacular entry doors, opposite. Adorned with leaded, faceted crystal in an intricate pattern, this is the best example of what is possible with the salt palette—wood, metallic fixtures, brass bells, black line work, and tints of varying whites.

SHADOW PLAY

A skylight casts a vivid shadow of black and white down on this bedroom, merging the two hues. Throughout the day this portal lets in light from all angles, moving the interest and focus around the room, and spontaneously changing the ratio of black, white, and gray. Architectural shapes are abundant in this palette when the light filters in.

GO BIG

Long Japanese rice paper scrolls with huge India ink paintings line the wall in my studio. Botanical silhouettes in black and white graphically represent nature beyond the boundaries of the walls. Never shy away from going supersize with artwork—it can make the whole room.

FLEA MARKETS

I can tell a lot about a region's history based on what I see in flea market and antique booths.

CALIFORNIA
Alameda Point Antiques Faire
www.alamedapointantiques
faire.com
2900 Navy Way
Alameda, CA 94501
510.522.7500
The largest antiques show in Northern California; it's grown wildly over the years.

FLORIDA
Lincoln Road Antique Market
www.antiquecollectiblemarket
.com
Lincoln Road Mall
Miami Beach, FL 33139
305.531.0038
Open on weekends, this one is full of 19th- to 20th-century collectibles. The best part is that the market is surrounded by palm trees. Anything is good near the beach!

GEORGIA
Scott Antique Markets
www.scottantiquemarket.com
3650 Jonesboro Road SE
Atlanta, GA 30354
404.361.2000
They claim to be "The World's Largest Monthly Indoor Antique Show." I pop over regularly for inspiration and a treasure or two.

INDIANA
Shipshewana Auction & Flea Market
www.tradingplaceamerica.com
345 S. Van Buren Street
Shipshewana, IN 46565
260.768.4129
The largest flea market in the Midwest with one hundred acres of booths all in one location.

MASSACHUSETTS
Brimfield Antique Show
www.brimfieldshow.com
60 Mt. Dan Road
Fiskdale, MA 01518
508.347.3929
The largest outdoor antique show in the world. A resource for every major design house in New York City. I like that there are tons of European antiques.

NEW YORK
The Annex Markets
Annex Antiques Fair & Flea Market
www.annexantiques.com
25th Street at 6th Avenue
West 39th Street at 9th Avenue
New York, NY 10001
New York City's best flea market. From African art to vintage clothing, I always walk away with a treasure. It was part of my weekend routine all the years I lived in Manhattan.

TENNESSEE
The 127 Corridor Sale
www.127sale.com
114 West Central Avenue
Jamestown, TN 38556
800.327.3945
The longest yard sale in the world—it starts in Michigan and ends in Alabama! You never know what you're going to find here. You can go for five miles or three hundred.

TEXAS
The Original Round Top Antiques Fair
www.roundtoptexasantiques.com
512.237.4747
Americana antiques at their finest—everything from old farm tools used as art to trunks and furniture. The fact that it's in Texas makes it more rustic. I've found incredible inspiration in the vintage books and ledgers from farms sold here.

NURSERIES

I like checking out nurseries whenever I visit a new city.

CALIFORNIA
Flora Grubb Gardens
www.floragrubb.com
1634 Jerrold Avenue
San Francisco, CA 94124
415.626.7256
This beautiful indoor/outdoor shop from an energetic young gardener always inspires.

GEORGIA
Goodness Grows
www.goodnessgrows.com
332 Elberton Road
Lexington, GA 30648
706.743.5055
Rick's nursery is a work of art—so much care and artistry go into these plants. They cultivate their own seedlings in special varieties and wouldn't even consider selling anything subpar.

NEW YORK
Saipua
www.saipua.com
147 Van Dyke Street
Brooklyn, NY 11231
718.624.2929
Extraordinary flower design and lovely handmade soaps.

PENNSYLVANIA
Terrain
www.shopterrain.com
914 Baltimore Pike
Glen Mills, PA 19342
610.459.2400
Terrain is gorgeous and run like a small business, despite the fact that it has a large parent company.

TEXAS

David Austin Roses
www.davidaustinroses.com
15059 State Highway 64 West
Tyler, TX 75704
800.328.8893
Like a dessert bar of roses. Over the years, my mother has given me all sorts of roses from here. They are amazing.

Lady Bird Johnson Wildflower Center
www.wildflower.org
4801 La Crosse Avenue
Austin, Texas 78739
512.232.0100
Lady Bird Johnson was responsible for beautifying highway medians and roadsides with wildflowers. This center is a way to experience all of her work and is full of gardening inspiration.

UK

Petersham Nurseries
www.petershamnurseries.com
Church Lane, off Petersham Road
Richmond, Surrey, UK
TW10 7AG
(0) 208.940.5230
An influential lifestyle nursery with breathtaking plants and objects.

SHOPS

It's fun to have a roster of shops that always inspire me.

CALIFORNIA

Bell'occhio
www.bellocchio.com
10 Brady Street
San Francisco, CA 94103
415.864.4048
This tiny shop sells my favorite Santa Maria Novella fragrance among other exquisite objects. The way they wrap sold items is otherworldly. This place was a haven for me when I lived in SF.

Britex
www.britexfabrics.com
146 Geary Street
San Francisco, CA 94108
415.392.2910
A gorgeous fabric store with a huge selection.

Fred Segal
www.fredsegal.com
420 & 500 Broadway
Santa Monica, CA 90401
310.458.8100
Always a great place to shop. Everything is right on-trend; you won't want to leave without something.

Lost + Found
www.lostandfoundshop.com
6320 Yucca Street
Los Angeles, CA 90028
323.856.5872
A very creative retailer; a collection of small diverse shops.

Maxfield
www.maxfieldla.com
8825 Melrose Avenue
Los Angeles, CA 90069
310.274.8800
Dark and moody, Maxfield's offers chic LA fashion.

OK
www.okthestore.com
8303 West Third Street
Los Angeles, CA 90048
323.653.3501
A perfectly curated gift shop.

Sal Beressi Fabrics
sanfranciscofabrics.com
1504 Bryant Street
San Francisco, CA 94103
415.861.5004
A treasure trove of vintage fabrics.

GEORGIA

Agora Vintage
www.ilicartagora.com
260 West Clayton Street
Athens, GA 30601
706.316.0130
A great spot for vintage treasure hunting. I've gotten Italian vintage sunglasses here but you may just as easily leave with a butterfly collection and a 1970s afghan.

Bungalow Classic
www.bungalowclassic.com
1197 Howell Mill Rd NW
Atlanta, GA 30318
404.351.9120
A fantastic home store with a beautiful point of view and lovely owners.

Double Dutch Press
www.doubledutchpress.com
1377 Prince Avenue
Athens, GA 30606
706.546.0994
Opened by local artists, this printmaking studio offers gifts, classes, and custom printing.

Jackson Street Books
260 N Jackson Street
Athens, GA 30601
706.546.0245
A big selection of used and new books.

Low Yo Yo Stuff Records
lowyoyo@mindspring.com
261 West Washington Street
Athens, GA 30601
Walk in to browse records or talk about the influence Fela Kuti had on New Orleans rap. They know everything about music. Really.

R Wood Studio
www.rwoodstudio.com
450 Georgia Drive
Athens, GA 30605
706.613.8525
The queen of Georgia pottery maintains this folkloric pottery studio, which is also a retail shop.

Treehouse Kid and Craft
www.treehousekidandcraft.com
815 W Broad Street
Athens, GA 30601
706.850.8226
Scandinavian-feeling shop for kids and the kid at heart. Filled with laughter coming from the daily craft classes for all ages.

MASSACHUSETTS

Good
www.shopatgood.com
133 Charles Street
Boston, MA 02114
617.722.9200
A beautifully curated store full of jewelry and home accessories.

NEW YORK

A Detacher
www.adetacher.com
262 Mott Street
New York, NY 10012
212.625.3380
My go-to store for chic clothing.

BDDW
www.bddw.com
5 Crosby Street
New York, NY 10013
212.625.1230
Famously talented woodsmen,
creating museum-quality
furniture designs.

Bird
www.shopbird.com
220 Smith Street
Brooklyn, NY 11201
718.797.3774
A gorgeous selection of fashion
from young designers.

Creatures of Comfort
www.creaturesofcomfort.us
205 Mulberry Street
New York, NY 10012
212.925.1005
A great shop showcasing fashion from a beautifully curated
selection of designers.

Dashwood Books
www.dashwoodbooks.com
33 Bond Street
New York, NY 10012
212.387.8520
Paradise for art-book shopping.

de Vera
www.deveraobjects.com
1 Crosby Street
New York, NY 10013
212.625.0838
A museum-like shop of curiosities done in the most luxuri-
ous way.

John Derian Company
www.johnderian.com
6 East Second Street
New York, NY 10003
212.677.3917
John's a kindred spirit, and I
love everything that he does. I
have so many things from his
shop in my home.

Kiosk
www.kioskkiosk.com
41 Union Square West #925
New York, NY 10003
212.226.8601
Worldly objects sourced from
the owners' exotic travels.

Makie
www.makieclothier.com
109 Thompson Street
New York, NY 10002
212.625.3930
Gorgeous Japanese clothing
for women and children. Spare
designs and simple silhouettes.

**Melet Mercantile Vintage
Showroom**
www.meletmercantile.com
84 Wooster St. #205
New York, NY 10012
212.925.8353
Melet is an ex-Ralph Lauren
vintage buyer. His aesthetic is
beyond words, and his store is
a haven for stylists.

Opening Ceremony
www.openingceremony.us
35 Howard Street
New York, NY 10013
212.219.2688
Wildly creative downtown
fashion.

Paula Rubenstein
www.paularubenstein.com
21 Bond Street
New York, NY 10012
212.966.8954
A mecca of unique curiosities.

Potterton Books
www.pottertonbooksusa.com
979 Third Avenue #101
New York, NY 10022
212.644.2292
My go-to store for rare
design books.

Steven Alan
www.stevenalan.com
158 Franklin Street
New York, NY 10013
646.402.9661
Smart, hipster fashions.

Ted Muehling
www.tedmuehling.com
52 White Street
New York, NY 10013
212.431.3825
Sculptural jewelry and objects
make this store a favorite for
the most fashionable collectors.

SOUTH CAROLINA
Worthwhile
www.shopworthwhile.blogspot.com
268 King Street
Charleston, SC 29401
843.723.4418
Perfectly-selected clothing and
gifts in a lovely French apothe-
cary atmosphere.

TEXAS
Bell + Bird
www.bellandbird.com
1206 West 38th Street #1102
Austin, TX 78705
512.407.8206
Inimitable jewelry collected
from estates and around the
globe make this special store
a visual treat.

JM Dry Goods
www.jmdrygoods.com
215 S. Lamar, Suite C
Austin, TX 78704
512.579.0303
A Texas vibe with California-
chic style in one of my favorite
cities.

Uncommon Objects
www.uncommonobjects.com
1512 S Congress Avenue
Austin, TX 78704
512.442.4000
This was my resource for found
beauty when we had two Hable
stores in NYC. Very distinctive
collections that will keep you
looking for hours.

WASHINGTON
Totokaelo
www.totokaelo.com
1523 10th Avenue
Seattle, WA 98122
206.623.3583
Amazing selection of fashion
and home wares with a strong
online shop.

UK
Cloth House, No. 47
www.clothhouse.com
188 Kensington Park Road
London, UK W11 2ES
(0) 323.549.9668
An oasis of fabric and remnants
in London.

Couverture
www.couvertureandthegarb
store.com
130 Royal College Street
Camden Town
London, UK NW1 0TA
(0) 207.485.6247
A gorgeous retailer of men's and
women's home goods with a
distinctive point of view.

Liberty
www.liberty.co.uk
Regent Street
London, UK W1B 5AH
(0) 207.734.1234
Liberty is king of beautiful
patterns. I love their fabric and
their store!

BOOKS AND PUBLICATIONS

Opening a book or magazine is one of the best ways to learn and get inspired.

And the Pursuit of Happiness and *The Principles of Uncertainty*, by Maira Kalman
Whimsical, current, and colorful. Her storytelling, excitement, and visions of history and culture make these books hard to put down.

Bloom magazine
www.edelkoort.com/trend_publication
The art of it! I've sought inspiration with this beautifully printed magazine for more than fifteen years. The entire archive is available online, but try to get your hands on a print copy!

Bonheur Automatique, by Hanspeter Hofmann
An artist's book, seemingly unending, dedicated to color and palette. It's about the creative process. I like that there's no beginning or end, and that he makes the book an object.

Color Moves: Art & Fashion, by Sonia Delaunay
I'm inspired by Sonia Delaunay's style and being—she didn't separate art from life and was brazen, confident, and smart. She was a go-getter who owned her own businesses. This book is an archive of her work in fashion and textiles.

Interaction of Color, by Josef Albers
"A record of an experimental way of studying color and of teaching color." —author Josef Albers. This book is an inspiring look at color combinations in a simple format.

Interiors, by Martyn Thompson
www.martynthompsonstudio.com
A photography book of artists' spaces. I love how Thompson sees the world. There's an aura around his photographs.

Kinfolk magazine
www.kinfolk.com
A lifestyle magazine with ethereal photography and beautiful printing.

The Native Trees of Canada, by Leanne Shapton
The pages of this book are filled with paintings of leaves from trees native to Canada. Shapton motivates me to not stay too long on a detail while I'm painting.

NY Book Art Fair
www.nyartbookfair.com
A great way to spot trends in art and publishing.

Selvedge magazine
www.selvedge.org
Textile love and an inside view of artists' studios. They dig around in obvious places, turning over stones that are always surprising.

The World of Interiors magazine
www.worldofinteriors.co.uk
Lovely, full of endless inspiration worth saving. Features a great mixture of designers, decorators, and real people.

The World of Madeleine Castaing, by Emily Evans Eerdmans
French interior designer and decorator Madeleine Castaing is an iconoclast. I cherish her unique voice.

A Yorkshire Sketchbook, by David Hockney
A collection of colorful sketches. This book reminds me to just relax. His brushstrokes are loose and quick—it's a reminder to not linger and to push forward toward the big picture. Thank you, David Hockney.

OTHER RESOURCES

CAUS
The Color Association of the United States
info@colorassociation.com
www.colorassociation.com
33 Whitehall Street, M3
New York, NY 10004
212.947.7774
An association of color consultants for global initiatives including product design and architecture. The company navigates the future of color.

The Design Library
info@design-library.com
www.design-library.com
400 Market Industrial Park, Suite 1
Wappingers Falls, NY 12590
845.297.1035
Beautifully curated resource comprised of patterns and textiles from many cultures and time periods.

Harvard Digital Collections Library
http://library.harvard.edu/digital-collections
A great online resource for inspiration from many cultures. The Emily Dickinson Herbarium is a favorite of mine for its color and form.

New York Public Library
Mid-Manhattan Library
www.nypl.org
455 Fifth Avenue (at 40th Street)
New York, NY 10016
212.340.0863
Endless resource of design motifs for any inspiration one may need.

CREDITS

The interior images in this book feature the home of Susan Hable and her family, except as noted below. We would like to thank our sweet friends near and far who allowed us to photograph their homes and spaces for this book.

PRIVATE HOMES

Rinne Allen and Lee Smith:
   Pages 58—59, 74—75, 158—159
Suzanne B. Allen Design, LLC:
   Pages 136, 186—187
Christy Bush: Pages 24, 33
Katherine and John Chaisson:
   Page 165

April Chapman:
   Pages 64, 100, 106
Liz and Tony Demarco:
   Pages 110, 134, 143, 195—196
Peggy and Denny Galis:
   Pages 76—77

Lucy and Jim Gillis: Pages 84,
   85, 126—27, 137, 145, 193
Carol John and Carl Martin:
   Pages 56, 61, 63, 86—87, 98,
   161, 168—169, 182, 197
Nancy Lendved:
   Pages 42, 84, 130—131, 164

Michael Stipe (apartment
   design by D.O.C., Unlimited):
   Pages 114, 119
Margie Spalding:
   Pages 43, 60, 109, 138, 167

PUBLIC SPACES

Athens Welcome Center at the
   Church-Waddell-Brumby
   House, Athens, Georgia:
   Pages 102—103, 111

Drayton Hall, Charleston, South
   Carolina: Pages 55, 184—185

House of Dance and Feathers,
   New Orleans, Louisiana:
   Pages 140—141

Mt. Zion, Sparta, Georgia:
   Pages 190—191

PAINT COLORS AND WALLPAPERS

Pages 18—19: Benjamin Moore
   1261, "Paisley Pink"
Page 21: Wallpaper: Jocelyn
   Warner, "Kaleido" in Pink
Pages 28—29: Farrow and Ball
   235, "Borrowed Light"
Pages 44—45: Wall color: Farrow
   and Ball 34, "Calke Green";
   Trim: Farrow and Ball 80,
   "Saxon Green"
Pages 54: Wallpaper: Brun-
   schwig & Fils, "Latrobe" in
   Seafoam (discontinued)

Page 56: Wall color:
   Ralph Lauren GH171,
   "Outrigger Orange"; Floor:
   Benjamin Moore 2120-60,
   "White Water"
Pages 58-59: Benjamin Moore
   AF-505, "Blue Echo"
Page 81: Wallpaper: Neue Gal-
   lery 69401-812, "Antinous"
   in Faun

Page 85: Wall color: Farrow and
   Ball 85, "Oval Room Blue";
   Trim: Benjamin Moore OC-8,
   "Elephant Tusk"
Pages 86—87: Floor: Benjamin
   Moore 2120-60, "White Water"
Page 104: Farrow and Ball 71,
   "Pale Hound"
Pages 126—127: Benjamin Moore
   HC-31, "Waterbury Cream"
Pages 140—141: Flavor Paper
   "Highway 66" in Pomegranate,
   on Chrome Mylar

Pages 152—153: Farrow and Ball
   92, "Castle Grey"
Page 156: Farrow and Ball 89,
   "Lulworth Blue"
Page 193: Benjamin Moore
   HC-169, "Coventry Gray"

ACKNOWLEDGMENTS

This book started out as a collection of different ideas three years ago and it has been exhilarating to watch it bloom. Literally and figuratively, the doors kept opening. I'm thankful to live in Athens, Georgia. In these pages you see the history, homes, light, and color that make this place so magical. Faces I knew and didn't know welcomed me. It's a great town that way.

I would not be living here if Lucy Gillis had not praised this community so wholeheartedly. Thank you, Lucy, for guiding me here and for your written contributions to the book.

Thank you to Rinne Allen for being so welcoming and nurturing. Your eye and sensitivity to natural light, color, and composition create an unmatched aura around your photos, and I can't imagine a better photographer for this book. I love seeing through your eyes and have enjoyed working with you so much through the years.

This project would never have seen the light of day without Chronicle Books. Publishing such gorgeous books is truly inspiring, and editor Laura Lee Mattingly's commitment to understanding what we wanted to say through photographs and color was invaluable. Thank you for supporting this project and for guiding us seamlessly through the process. And thank you to the rest of the Chronicle Books team who worked so diligently to make this dream a reality: Allison Weiner, Mikayla Butchart, Sara Golski, Stephanie Wong, Steve Kim, and Yolanda Cazares.

I am so very grateful to the homeowners who allowed me into their dwellings: Rinne Allen and Lee Smith, Christy Bush, April Chapman, Liz and Tony Demarco, Peggy and Denny Galis, Lucy and Jim Gillis, Brian Hitselberger and Bill Cottrell, Carol John and Carl Martin, Nancy Lendved, Margie Spalding, Michael Stipe, Drayton Hall, the Athens Welcome Center, Suzanne Allen and Randy Taylor, Lamar Wood, Cassie and David Bryant, and Katherine and John Chaisson.

A great group of creative people were excited about this book from the start and helped all along the way. Hope Hilton's incredible way of collecting the words that I stumble to say comes easily to her. Thank you for being the other eyes to our project. I'm also thankful for Kathleen Hendricks's meticulous eye, Rebecca's Ennis's enthusiasm, and for the assistance of Eunice, Brooke, and Sydney, our Hable interns. Chrissy Reed and Michelle Norris assisted Rinne along the way, and we are lucky to have worked with them. Over the years, Hable has created relationships with many helpers to make it all happen: screenprinters, sewers, and manufacturers in the United States who have supported our business from the beginning. Members of the Hable team through the years who have gotten us to where we are now, thank you for the many moves, wild ideas, and hard work. Thank you to Amy Brookshire for your heart and support. My dear friend, John Derian, thank you for your love.

My deepest affection goes to my husband, Pete, my caretaking tiger. Thank you for the years of unconditional support and proudly living in a pink house. For always embracing my changes, quietly watching me grow, and watching me regularly evolve as I do. My children Bird and Lake bring such energy and joy to my days. Your uncensored opinions and observations enlighten me regularly, and your quick wit and creativity make me honored to be your mother.

Katharine Hable Sweeney, without you I wouldn't have the pleasure of pursuing my dreams. Your unconditional trust, encouragement, and support—of my art especially—has made this all possible. I am lucky to have a partner like you with whom I can weather the fun yet trying times of running a small creative business. You're my mainstay, my sister, and my friend. I'm so grateful for you.

Thank you to my parents, Kay and Paul, for encouraging me to experience life and all of its offerings, to travel even if I only had two nickels to rub together, and to succeed. No words can describe how truly thankful I am to have you as my mom and dad.

This is only the beginning.